THE BLUE MOUTH OF MORNING

The Blue Mouth Of Morning

POEMS BY

Harold Rhenisch

OOLICHAN BOOKS
LANTZVILLE, BRITISH COLUMBIA, CANADA
1998

Canadian Cataloguing in Publication Data

Rhenisch, Harold, 1958-

 The blue mouth of morning

 Poems.

ISBN 0-88982-173-9

I. Title.

PS8585.H54B68 1998   C811'.54   C98-910949-6
PR9199.3.R464B68 1998

We gratefully acknowledge the support of the Canada Council for the Arts
for our publishing program.

THE CANADA COUNCIL | LE CONSEIL DES ARTS
FOR THE ARTS | DU CANADA
SINCE 1957 | DEPUIS 1957

Grateful acknowledgement is also made to the BC Ministry of Tourism, Small
Business and Culture for their financial support.

We acknowledge the financial support of the Government of Canada
through the Book Publishing Industry Development Program for our
publishing activities.

Cover image: Chuckchee Star map from the papers of Waldemaar Bogoros.
Used with permission of University of Washington Special Collections
Library.

Published by
Oolichan Books
P.O. Box 10, Lantzville
British Columbia, Canada
V0R 2H0

Printed in Canada by
Morriss Printing Company
Victoria, British Columbia

in memory of
Charles Lillard
1944-1997
and Robin Skelton
1925-1997

Acknowledgements

Canadian Literature: The Deciphering of the Code of Time
Event: Home on the Range, The Sphere

The Lesson, Space and Time, The First Day, The Baroque Cupola, The Art Nouveau Window, The Renaissance Confessional Boxes, and The Present Time were finalists in the CBC/Saturday Night/Tilden Literary Competition (1995 and 1996).

The author wishes to thank the British Columbia Arts Council for a grant which enabled him to complete this book.

Contents

The New Land

The Real Work

Coyote works hard,
unstringing the barbed wire
from the fences on the plateau
and herding the cattle out at night
while ranchers swim helplessly
far out at sea.

Some nights Coyote is content
to nip at heels
as cattle thunder
and bellow through marsh grass,
burrs catching in their hair.

On other nights he dresses carefully
in turquoise and black
leather chaps edged with silver,
with boots of rattlesnake and fish skin,
dons a sweeping hat with many tassels,
and is ready just before dawn.

As a cold night wind flows
through bunchgrass and poplars,
a late moon breaks and floods
along the edge of the sky;
Coyote mounts the herd bull,
and sitting on the rippling muscles
of the great beast's white neck,
grabs its horns, and rides
through the ranchyards
singing old songs passed down
by his family in Chihuahua.

Those are the mornings when the ranchers sense him,
for when the green-feathered roosters crow,
the ranchers step onto their verandas,
hear music and see the air ripple
as if their cattle are passing through it.

Sometimes Coyote ties pink and yellow feathers
to the tips of the bulls' horns,
dresses in his own skin
and sits demurely on the backs of the cows
as they follow the bulls out into the world.

Sometimes Coyote does not touch the barbed wire.
Those are the nights when he dresses in gold
and carries a red cape over his shoulder.
Those are the nights when he steps
into the ranchers' dreams, flares the cloth suddenly,
and once the ranchers charge after him—
to discover they have no guns there, in their dreams—
whips the cloth away,
and vanishes back into the dark
where they will never find him.

It is this moment Coyote longs for
and has been working towards continuously.

When it comes
he sits on top of a pile of round bales
and squirms with excitement,
listening with an ear cocked
for what might happen then.

The Language of Silence

Among the wild strawberries in the clearcut
next to a shallow stream

I am left to speak with horses

They carry Plato's furniture on their backs
In the drawers of the commodes
carefully folded in silk
are their memories

The horses know about balance

Memory is my country
With each passing year it has weighed on me more heavily

and now I speak with horses

it has taken me forty years to come to this

Red ants scurry over the horses' flanks
as we talk

There is a stillness to the air
It is as if a school of trout
muscular and cold
cat-like

are slipping through trunks
and over my hands

Home on the Range

In June Mozart moves out to the range
and rides the bulls as they slip, black,
through white-trunked aspens. As he rides,
he sings arias under his breath,
old Hank Williams songs from the radio,
and something new, a kind of music
that sounds like starlight blowing through trees
and coyotes yipping from stone-dry arroyos.

In the height of summer he brings the bulls down
from the rangeland to the city. In a dusty field
between the railroad and the lumber yards,
cowboys ride his bulls for money and fame.

Mozart dresses as a clown.
When a cowboy is thrown,
he steps in the bull's path
and sings arias from Don Giovanni
and the Barber of Seville.
While the cowboy scrambles away, the bull
nuzzles Mozart's hand for a cube of sugar.

Mozart has trained the cows as well;
when he rides on the shoulders of the lead bull,
back up the silver rivers and red stone washes
into the rangeland, the cows stand with their calves
among the trees, singing in chorus.

As the stars flow and swirl
in vast currents overhead, the gold
gradually settles out
in the deeper pools, until slowly,
over the shoulder of the land,
it is day—and the clouds tower over the forests
all the way to the sea.

The Scent of the Earth

Coyote has answered one of those real estate ads
for a lakeshore farm in the high country
with a view off the edge of the plateau
to the mountains
cloaked in blue shadow and white glaciers,
against whose slopes clouds form
like breath on a winter morning—

and he is a farmer now
according to the custom
of the land. Today he has hooked up the tractor
to an old two-bottom plough. As the diesel
exhaust spills over his face
and leaves fall, a yellow avalanche
as thick as February snow,
he ploughs his fields
into the black waves of the sea.

In the cool of dusk, when the air is pale lavender,
he cuts the throttle and walks
across the furrows in sudden hammering silence,
his hands smelling of his leather gloves,
until he sees the first star
rise above the glacier.

As the frost settles out of the quartz air,
he sits on the bare black soil,
waiting for the first fish to rise
from the glacial stones.

By midnight, all the old roofs of the farm,
the white poplars,
the distant peaks, and the faces of the furrows
glow with the silver light of fish,
and Coyote rises and calls. And the fish come

slowly, impossibly, out of the land,
bucking, heaving,
and breaking free,
swimming down the cut sods,
out through the neighbouring meadows
of wheatgrass and sedges,
and into the sky.

It is a form of farming
which brings no monetary return
and produces no produce for sale
or even for consumption,
and although Coyote had to mortgage himself for years
down in the valleys
to purchase the farm, he does not allow himself to think
that he owns this land: he is simply glad
to be able to return it to the sky
and to sit all night in the scent of the earth.

A Second Chance for Helios

108 Mile Ranch

The swallows are weaving
the evening light. The male
carries on his back a small
golden man with a whip and halter.

In her bill the female
carries the remnants
of a golden chariot,
twisted and bent.

They fly under the eaves
of an old hand-notched barn
as the lake flares at its feet—
a wind, broad and green.

As they plunge into the hayloft,
Helios has a glimpse
through the floorboards
to the steaming backs

of the giant Clydesdales
in their dark, hay-rich stalls.
They raise great moon eyes,
framed by seafoam,

at the sudden glint of gold. That
is how Helios remembers them.
He remembers them all summer
as the beginning of the world—

while he grows in a mud nest
tucked under a drumming steel roof
into a small bird the colour of a beetle
flashing out of pines into yellow light,

long after the sun
has entered the clouds
and fallen like thunder
beneath the edge of the world.

The Hidden One

Hedley

The ravens write with their claws in the snow.
I walk through the junk: I can't read a thing.
The king stands proudly on an old mattress.

He has found a piece of rusted steel
and is using it for a voice. His calls
echo off the smoke-blackened cliffs. His band
call to him like politicians: self-effacing and loud.

They have a big secret: they have found a small
clot of self-consciousness in a tomato sauce tin—
it is enough for the lot of them.

But I am not a politician. I turn
amid the filth to look at the king
once more. His wings are two metres broad.

He glides slowly over the writing;
my footsteps lead illegibly through it,
breaking the sentences apart. The king screams.

Landing, he scratches a new sentence in the snow.
He looks like something that he found here—
or something he lost. He stands motionless,
a black period, and stares at me. I stare back.

In the clear light between us, above
the filthy soil, quivers the consciousness,
which we both at the same time
gently and wonderingly touch.

It doesn't make a sound.

Seductions

My grandmother kept a salamander in her mouth;
when she spoke the room was set on fire.
In the age of steel and despair she was a doctor
who threw huge parties in her rose garden
for industrialists and military men.

The maids poured wine in moonlight;
the sounds of laughter trickled into darkness
on a yellow river of candles and cut glass.
When my grandmother toasted the moon,
the salamander drank greedily.
the golden wine flew down its throat like rain.

After the party the scent of warm wine floated:
a curtain drawn by frightened fingers.
My grandmother stared over the roses
and the canal behind them, totally sober,
while the salamander who lived within her
slept, dreaming of a golden world.

Those were the years of emptiness
which slid quickly into the years of war.
The salamander moved down to the canal.
You could see him as the morning sun struck the water,
granting it shape and form. You could see him
in the sun flooding the hospital windows
and holding there, flowing no further,
whole walls of bound light, trembling.

A year later, my grandmother sheltered a French prisoner
in the wineroom, while at the same time war
embraced her, sobbing, *History is our seduction.*

There was nowhere to turn.

The Nazi Doctor

My grandfather was a doctor.
He worked with the dogs of hell;
his operating theatre was knee deep in snow.
He ate white pills;
he bathed his face in blood.

When the German army took Warsaw,
my grandfather was there.
The other officers were housed in golden halls
with paintings of cherubs set into the plaster of the ceilings
between carved white trunks of trees, but my grandfather,
who had been a heart surgeon in the city of cathedrals,
slept on a gurney to one side of the operating room
while young men bled around him;
when he saw flowers sprout in shellholes
they might as well have been on the moon.

The cathedral in my grandfather's city is famous for its spire,
which narrows halfway up then flares again slightly—
an impossible feat of engineering—
yet it still stands.

When Minsk fell, my grandfather was there,
his hands buried in the chests of dying young men.
When Odessa fell, men were brought to him,
burnt black like trees
after a lightning fire has surged across the ridges,
leaping from crown to crown,
driven by wind—

my grandfather spent five years
with his fingers on the beating hearts of young men,
the same fingers he had once used to play the piano
above the rose garden in his villa
in the muddy town
where he had left his children to run wild.

When Minsk was retaken, my grandfather was in the last convoy out,
walking through the rubble,
pointing to men lying wrapped in grey blankets, saying,
"This one should live; this one has no chance,"
and leaving the dying to the Russians,
who shot them out of hand.

This war was of my grandfather's making,
yet when Odessa was liberated
he did not know it; he was lying on a blood-soaked bed
under the fingers of a Russian surgeon,
who rebuilt three vertebrae with silver
and set a silver plate in the back of his skull;

when he woke from the sedative
he was unable to move and did not know his name.

The music he most loved to play was Beethoven;
he claimed Beethoven was his soul;
it was unlike any other music—although he also played
Chopin with great verve, as he had first heard it in his childhood
in Poland.

Behind his house water flowed out of the Black Forest
and the feet of the old robber castle,
into the heavy industrial Rhine. In that house
he dreamed of Goethe and his simple songs
of women becoming roses. It was not a metaphor.

All my life I have lived without a grandfather. This afternoon
I see the cathedral, where the Gauleiters were christened,
where the books were burned,
where Heidegger ran the university for men
in tall black leather boots,
who ran from public buildings to their waiting cars,
for even in power they feared assassination.

The cathedral was built by a knight
who ate his enemies with great ceremony,
in the city that never housed a Jew,
where the last witch in Europe was burned.
It is a hollow crypt of stone, the golden altar
at the heart of the cross, the choir in the loft like angels,
powered by breath.

My grandfather was there in the snow outside Moscow,
stalked by wolves among exploding birch trees,
the light so thin the stars were never absent from the air,
where a man's breath froze directly in front of him
and fell to his feet like an admonition.

It was not a message.
As the bell tolls in the tower, and the bookstore
at its feet sells old Party newspapers,
I know what my grandfather had to say about

submission.

Departures

A wind blows quietly through poppies.
Grandma's hips are fragile as glass.
She sweats and eats ice cream
with the other wheelchair riders.
They stare out the big windows
at the beech trees, the tennis court
and its floor of red clay: what's left
of old bricks from the years after the war.
When the young men and women hit the ball,
the sound spills unheard among the tables
in the eternal coolness of glass.

As the tower of the Church of Mary,
rising in the heat above
the black and red roofs of the old city
looms over my shoulder
through the door
of the train station, I leave this city
in which my grandfather, the military doctor,
started a new practice among the rich
after he had lost everything,
especially the naiveté of his youth.
Now it is peach harvest.
Sweating, I stare out the train window
at the small gardens planted among the tracks,
while Grandma sleeps,
every moment farther away,
drunk on ice cream.

Paradise Found

Back in the '50s Shakespeare used to run a skidder
out of Anaheim Lake,
but now he's opened a lawnmower repair shop
amidst the old singlewides and rusty Chevrolets of Lac La Hache,
and charges by the hour. The walls of his shop
are plastered with sonnets, printed in the pale colours
of the '40s, the paper yellowed with the years.
The floor is dirt packed hard as cement,
littered with old greasy gears,
piston heads, and shining carburetor needles.
Shakespeare is in the back by the grinder,
a blue welder's cap covering his skinny bald head,
a spray of sparks shooting around him
while he grinds the slag off a half-molten piston
to the tune of the low-pitched roar
that sinks off the stone.

Down the highway from Shakespeare's Lawnmower Repair
John Milton, whose eyesight has been restored
by swimming through the river of silence,
has settled his daughters in a fly-tying shop.
There is nothing fancy here, and nothing is arranged for tourists,
but John has been fishing in Lac La Hache and Rail Lake
and the glacial and horsefly country of the Chilcotin
for sixty years and has learned a thing or two
in that time.

Most any day you will find him in an old Coors Lite T-Shirt,
a pot-belly hanging over his jeans,
peering over the tops of his bifocals
at delicate watercolours of chironomids and mayflies
that look like fairies, that look able to grace us

with a love more intense than cut flowers,
and which he painstakingly copies with deerhide, coloured thread
and wood-duck feathers.

If you want to find his daughters
you will have to canoe onto the lake,
for they spend their days there,
clear-skinned, scooping the latest hatch off the water,
where wings gleam white
against the deep without light,
thoughts floating on the first age of the world;
and paint them on heavy rag paper
with handmade sow's bristle brushes.

This is their share of the work now,
and after his passage through blindness
John is glad of it.

On Mondays John hangs the closed sign in the front window
and goes onto the lake with his neighbour.
In the middle of the lake, Shakespeare cuts the old Evinrude
and they drift with the slow current;
he drops a line with lead weights and a lurid
pink and green plug over the stern
and is content to lie back
watching the pattern of the clouds
drift across the gentian sky, but Milton is not.
He stands in the prow
and with deft flicks of his wrist
casts a fly far out onto the still black
ahead of them, into absolute emptiness,
into the pure definition of water,
and with trembling fingers and a pounding heart
waits for a fish to rise and strike hard.

Plato's Penance

Plato has given up on the just order
of life among men;
with breath rich from Player's tobacco
and fingers orange from hand-rolled cigarettes,
he runs a timber-cruising company
out of Williams Lake.

His office is the front room
of a fifty-year-old clapboard house,
in the fly-ash from the mill
and the hammering of the night trains.

In the blue-and-white television flicker
he sits on his Naugahyde couch,
his papers spread around him,
charting the timber of cut-blocks
in the sacred land spoken
at the beginning of the world.

He will admit readily
he once tried to fashion a world based on exclusion
and the manipulation of thought
through embodiments of rhetoric
in the forms of the world.

He will apologize: If you visit,
he will sweep aside the styrofoam cups,
turn down the volume,
and out of bleary eyes

as grey as the distant sea
tell how in the Chilcotin
he almost lost his head to a trip wire
laid to catch wild horses
that eat grass which otherwise could be grazed
by cattle.

He was riding skidoo,
checking out the parameters of a stand—
lodgepole pine mostly,
a few firs and aspens by the lakes—
when he went down.

The horses are quartered with chainsaws,
hauled to town in pickups,
and sold as pet food. As Plato speaks,
you see in his eyes the mares
running wild across the eastern slopes,
their copper manes flowing.
Very pointedly Plato returns to his calculations—
the number of cubic feet per hectare.
In his eyes the green crowns of the trees
surge in a deep wind off the sea.

Sometimes Plato goes for breakfast at the all-night hotel.
He stays all morning smoking in the café
with a view of his old legacy,
the BC Rail switching yard,
full of coal cars and lumber cars heading south.
Because he can make no sense of his shame,
when the bar opens at noon
he goes in and watches women
strip down to their certainty.

He once wrote of cicadas,
women singing from hot stones,
memory—stripped from us—
given to the mute things of this earth.
At night he returns home
to work, his mind drenched with horses.

The Magician

in mem. Robin Skelton, 1925-1997

1. Greeting

An old man who lives in the city,
who has not trimmed his beard for twenty years,
came to me last night, his face ecstatic,
his head shaven, wearing black leather,
only a G-string between his buttocks.
He looked a man who had learned to see
into the scent of flowers, who had already left

to swim in a blue lake with wild roses
blooming along the shore; whose body
lingered like the low red light of evening
that breaks over the horizon and slowly vanishes,
an eye opened and shut once it has seen.
He had with him two young men who did not see
that he had become a creature of light,

a wild-eyed watcher who once stepped out of cedars
on the inlet shores and called to the sun
to rise out of drumming waves, flapping
its huge wings. To the young men he was only
that what they saw: a man wise with physical strength.
As he turned, leading them down a dark hall,
he laughed and his eyes burned.

One glance from his eyes was greeting for a lifetime.

2. Farewell

After his son died in fire,
the poet wrote a note of farewell:

We may live in paradise,
but we live there alone.

He was in the process of packing
his life into a black cardboard suitcase
and moving into the thorn forests,
taking with him everything of value—
a green parrot, a round ball of glass
thrown out by the sea, a two-foot-tall
wooden skeleton with a bird trilling
on its shoulder, and twirling a black cane,

but no papers and no books.

At night I find myself looking for him.
The scent of roses is thick on the air.
I hear the growl of giant cats; twigs break.

The search is made in darkness.
Some nights I am a pool in a clearing.
I look up and see his face. His hair is tangled
and tattered. The moon hunts him like a beast.

Some nights I am the trees. I hear him
breathe hard as he pushes through me.

Some nights I am the tiger; I am the dark.

It has been two years since my friend
learned that magic does not heal the world;
it only heals that which holds health within.

Now it is time to be the forest looking into the pool.

3. Greeting.

It is time to say goodbye to the poet.

His tongue was a leaf.

In his hands were the wings of a bird.

In his chest was a white stone temple
on a promontory above the sea.

In his eyes he felt the water foam and break.

In his eyes a woman watched the rising moon.

He was once a bird,
perched on an apple bough,
calling for rain.

Now his fingers are filled with pebbles.
They rattle as he walks.

There is thunder above the escarpment.

He was once a clown juggling in a pied tent,
while children laughed in fear.

The wild sorghum is as tall
as a woman dressed in sequins and feathers
and balanced on a man's shoulders;
it bends and breaks before the wind.

He was once a salmon
swimming up the Fraser
into the high evergreen forests,
the flat mountain lakes reflecting the sky
and the source of story.

Now his tongue flutters on its stem
and beads with the first drop of rain.

The poet is dying.

Molecule by molecule, he is being
replaced by motes of light.

Soon he will be only a stream of light
through the window
in the afternoon,

rising and setting
in intensity
as the day rises
and falls.

He has become the sea, the old mother,
the name of the self, the window
on the moon, and we cannot follow,

who have followed, and cannot look
for answers, who have asked.

The poet is becoming a certainty.

I push a boat from shore, through a forest
of kelp and darting fish into open water

and the first word of the world. Thunderheads
build on the horizon. Tonight
in the mountains it is going to rain,

and the trees will flutter and rise up.

Return to Open Water

Charles Lillard, 1944-1997

The whales call from the traffic
and Red comes to ride them
with a halter made of an old winch cable
He speaks to them in Chinook
In his pocket he carries a handful of trade beads
which he has promised to the Beaufort Sea

As the whales buck along Douglas Street
Red stands on the back of the lead whale
the cable cinched tightly around his left wrist
his right hand held out for balance
clutching a weatherbeaten hat like a young kid
at Anaheim Lake in July
When the traffic stalls at the Fort Street light
the exhaust pours over him like morning fog
over the herring beds
and he steadies his foothold
and holds on

As the whales pass through the downtown core
bucking and swaying
the cod begin to rise out of the alleys and loading zones
the herring descend in great shoals from the clouds
and the salmon slip out of the plate glass
They all flow down through the apartments of James Bay
the daffodils and gorse
picking up cod and mackerel bream and surf perch
then stream into the Strait of Juan de Fuca
and West through the brass gates which Drake saw there
marking the end of the world and the entrance of Eldorado

Red is not going to Eldorado
Red is going to sea

*

In Eldorado
we dress in gold
We deck our hair in feathers
dipped in pollen
We rub clay on our cheeks
Day and night the foundries
spark with molten gold
and the hammering of the goldsmiths
pours down every street
Books are brought in from the forest
where they have changed themselves
into birds
to hide from the fires
at the end of the world
And our goldsmiths
hammer them out flat
into the rain
into the scales of salmon
the eyes of halibut
staring out of the floor
of the sea

Red has them in his pocket
loose change for his voyage

We stand on shore
our golden clothes sparkle
in the sun
our turquoise rings
glow on our fingers

like eyes turned blind
eyes that can only
see the earth

*

A man stands in my doorway.
His body is fire.

I dress him in wind. He becomes the rain.

I dress him in rain. He becomes the sun.

I dress him in sun. He becomes the grass.

I dress him in grass. He becomes the wind.

Blowing away all memory.

Blowing away all rain,
all sun, all grass.

Blowing away.

No man stands
in my doorway.

I do not wake.
I have become the sea.

everyone is agitated.

The Centre

The Ancient Way

for Robin Skelton

There is a yellow stone
buried beneath the field.

There is a snake
curled around the rim of the world.

There is a field of grass;
the head of every stalk is a star.

There is a green trout
swimming in the sky.

There is a lion among the trees,
carved from stone,

painted the blue of morning;
his mane is fire.

It is not to be understood.
It is to be entered through the silence

on the far side of language
separating one word from the next,

the air between the trees
in a forest.

The 1936 Olympic Stadium

Garmisch-Partenkirchen. 1995

In a city of sulphur and glaciers,
stone men and women twelve feet tall
hold stone torches and challenge all takers
to climb the salt ladders of rain
into their eyes. Clouds build
against the broken walls of the world,
drive forward and vanish. Ants crawl
in long columns up the windows.

The giants walk through dark streets,
dropping one stone leaf of laurel
before each house. At dawn
mourning cloak butterflies fly west
in a vast cloud a hundred miles wide,
the trees sleep in their shadows, and people
open their broad doors. They pick
the leaves from their steps
and bring them in, glowing. The trees
are thick with small yellow birds.

As the first light strikes the branches,
the birds flush with a clear, high-pitched music
and a river flows from the mouth of a child
into the body of a violin
made by hand
out of snow.

The Sphere

You could eat these apples until late in the evening.
Everyone thinks everyone else is already asleep,
but they are behind curtains eating apples
from the south. On the trees outside, the apples
are still small and bright green. Everyone is excited:
they don't believe in the clouds painted in old churches,
nor in the dark brown houses of their city,
only in apples, that are delivered crisp and juicy
to their small shops from the other side
of the world. Because of apples like that you could forget
the way it is with people while they sleep.
Because of apples like that you could forget a lot:
you don't need a bed anymore; you don't need dreams.
Outside, the hard green apples look like small birds.
You wait for them to start singing. You sing a few
stanzas ahead of time, to teach them.
You just know the world is a sphere. It hangs on a tree.

The Lesson

Obersteinberg

In the village of the sun
the door of every house has a polished brass mirror.
The streets are dust. In the spring,
when the sun is snow, the children
are covered in mud. Their parents believe the sun is a mirror;
that because of the mirrors of their doors
their town is much warmer than the sun.
In the shadows of their schoolrooms,
in the flickering shade of oil lamps,
the children are taught that all light
comes from the moon. The insides of their houses
are cold. The children believe that the sun is a golden bird;
that you can see your face in a mirror.
It takes many years to teach them the truth.
Often their parents find them running without a hat
in the street. Again and again
and again their mothers explain
that the sun will make them cold,
that their houses will soon be covered
with the ice fields of the moon,
and again and again and again
their fathers cuff them behind the ears.

It is a hard lesson to learn.

Space and Time

Freiburg im Breisgau

What they know is stone.
In the middle of their city
which glows like coals in the evening sun,
where neither the still of the forest
nor the roar of the river is heard,
they have built a huge machine of red sandstone
to capture space and hold it
until the world is no more. Every day they step
through heavy steel doors
and stand very still in that space
to listen to the sound of absolute emptiness
which is also the sound of the mind working

while the river flows over weirs
like fine hand-woven lace.
Every day men climb the towers
and over the steep slate roof
to replace the stones and tiles that have cracked
and broken with time: in this way
they maintain the space
men and women of their city
captured seven hundred years ago.
It takes all their effort
but they do their work gladly,
for it is the only work there is in the world.

The Baroque Cupola

Today nobody goes anywhere by foot.
The men fly over the roofs. The women
swim through the narrow streets,
around the fountains, in the door of the church,
and out of the highest windows. Children
swim lightly on the clouds and sunbeams,
like geese and ducks. Life
is sometimes boring in the high mountains.
For eight weeks now there's been nothing but a hot white sun
that has drifted in the streets like snow,
but now there is rain.
No-one's going anywhere on foot.

A hand stands on the eave of a roof,
flapping like a wing. A farmer stands under it and calls
that he won't be able to bring the hay in
until it flutters down like a butterfly
and settles on the grass stem of his arm,
slowly waving its fingers.

People dress in cotton and candlelight. They listen
with beating hearts to the songs of the black firs
high in the mountains where the streams are poured
into small green bottles and delivered
everywhere by convoys of trucks in the night.
In the mountains the water no longer flows.
You climb slowly up the valleys, over the silver stones,
until you reach the cliffs. You lay your cheek on the hot stone,
and feel the heaviness of the world.

Soldiers of a foreign power, dressed in civilian clothes,
stroll everywhere. They are unseen. They have found a door,
and walk into gilded halls and step back out again
under trees full of wind.

Ravens stand in the grain fields. They scream,
slowly. They have voices of iron.
Their words are old, rusted nails
that children dig up in a garden.
Still more ravens leap off the towers of Heaven,
and fall like ashes to the ground.

But these are all old stories.

Today the wind is blue. Men and women
have faces as yellow as chalk. The children are purple.
As the wind blows through the narrow green alleys,
young women see their voices flash
up over the rooftops: a flock of starlings fluttering
out of a wheatfield into the flaming Autumn sun.

The Art Nouveau Window

in mem. Georg Trakl, 1887-1914

It was once so.

One evening a cow stepped from the underbrush
into a newly-mown meadow
where there were no trees.

She walked slowly,
as a heavy brass bell
that hung to her knees
off a leather collar
slowly tolled.

With every footstep
dandelions sprang from the soil.
By the time she stepped into the next forest,
the meadow was glowing brightly
in the long rays of the evening sun,

as if a giant lion
that had been sleeping under the earth
had awoken and looked around,
then slowly started to climb out of the ground
with stars in its mouth
and its eyes filled with milk.

And the world began.

Then it was over.

A dog is walking along the black path
into the potato field.

The stars flicker.
A woman wearing a red dress stands in a stone doorway
and stares the blue stars in the face.
A swamp wind howls through the daisy meadows.
A bell tolls in a ruined church by the river.
Its notes are the silver of fish. They swim heavily
through brown air; the stars go out; nothing burns.
The woman has vanished. The moon falls. The dog begins to run.

Tonight the dead have climbed out of the swamps
to graze on the small blue winter stars. Whenever they breathe,
fog freezes on the watery glass of the windows.
I dream that I am pushing my way through deep snow.
I wake with the moon in my mouth. It barks
in the middle of the desert of space as if a thousand
tiny insects were taking the house apart piece by piece.
In the middle of the forest the firs are flying away,
carrying the earth in their claws.

On the rim of the world a yellow horse runs
with a cock on its back.

The earth is a flame,
even heavier than the flame of wood.

We are burning.

The Renaissance Confessional Boxes

When I was still a small child, I had no skin at all;
every movement of the wind flowed directly into my blood. In Autumn,
when fish threw themselves out of the white lakes into the air,
I shivered with cold, for carried by the current of the wind, the stars
had settled in my bones. My fingers glowed with the tongues of birds.
The doctors had no answers. They tried to sew me a skin: leaves,
plastic, paper, cotton, leather and parachute nylon would not stick
and fell to the ground. After that, the doctors
went back to their field hospitals with trembling fingers,
and left me to find my own cure.

Underneath an apple tree I found an old book of poetry
and discovered a skin in there, while blue birds
flew through the leaves. This skin was strong
and thin, supple and full of colours, was sewn out of frogs
and flies, clouds and the motion of wind over the water
of a glacial lake. It fitted me perfectly.
For many years now I have worn this skin with pride—
whether I have stood in a grey city or on a mountain—
and everyone has noticed that a wind stood before them,
cool and damp. Now I look at old pictures in my album
and notice, shaken, that one is of a stranger, smiling,
another is of the moon, in another yellow leaves
lie on wet black soil under poplars while the sun
turns into a snow cloud—in yet another
there is snow, nothing more.

The sun lies on the bottom of the sea,
drinks water, shapes it into eggs of light,
and buries them in gravel.

The wind is a tree.

Now I am trying to take off this skin, but there are no buttons,
and it does not tear. Without pride I have to say
that I am my skin that I found in an old book of poetry; that when I page
through the album now, in the purple and blue shadowed snow,
I find nothing except the moon, the sun, and the world
that I must slowly, word by word, build out of the invisible,

so that there are still pictures.

The Present Time

Bochum

The deer have migrated from the forests
to the city. They wear daisies in their antlers
and sleep in a playground
near a connector street. Is there not anyone
who knows how to ride a deer,
with a golden horn and green eyes
stolen from a fairy as it looked into the mirror
of a forest pool? Yes. There are people
like that everywhere, but they are sleeping under a spell.

In the afternoon a truck pulls up, piled high with hay. A man
climbs down and throws the sweet-smelling
dried grass onto the playground sand
and sits there, thoughtfully, at peace,
while the deer step out of the hedges
and shyly taste the hay,

and cars stream by loudly on the street,
swallowing the air, their headlights burning.

The First Day

Hausberg

In one town in the white mountains
all the women have red hair.
They say the people there were foxes
when the world was made
of beech bark, the fluff of wild flower seeds
and dew, and that across the gorge
all the people were wild sheep
with long horns curled to the back
as they clattered over the sharp stones.

No one knows for sure,
yet in the town of foxes
the houses are made of lime
and on the stone threshold of every house
lies a dog. People say
that one night in the spring the trees
walk down from the mountains
into the streets, and rustle, dark and grey,
so thick that no-one can pass by or through.

No-one knows when,
but there was once a winter of heavy snow
after a summer of heavy rain
and in the spring the trees all bloomed
so brightly that the petals opened
with a sound like a small stone
that falls through the air
from a high cliff and there is no record
of its falling anywhere.

Waiting for the End of the World

In a city of fire someone is water;
doves are folded out of newspaper;
men work in a factory of dust and sweat;
the tongue is a hot coal.

In a city of fire, people keep bees:
they are drops of gold; they gather the sun,
that has been sown over the whole earth.
There are ants everywhere.

They step through fire without noticing it at all.
In the evenings it grows dark.
A wind of smoke roars through the streets.

Then women lay their heads on the shoulders of their men
and stare out their windows. The ants cross the streets
in long columns. They glow red in the last light,
that cuts sharply over the earth
and illuminates them brightly.

Even late in the night they are still glowing.

A New Music

Salzburg

Listening to Mozart at the Millennium

Salzburg is nothing.
It is the place where harmony is a river, running underground.
I live in the night. I have a broken vision
of golden grass lifting and falling in wind.
The inside of a stone speaks the stars tonight, as a fine snow
drifts over the frozen lake. This is Salzburg.

*

I left once. I urged the driver on;
we passed down the river to Vienna
and the king. The fields were green.
I travelled with a clown,
a countess in a purple dress,
and a hunter with an iron knife.
As we rolled down the night road, stars fell into the fields.
I smelled the river: salt. Wolves
ran soundlessly through the willows.
I called up to the coach man, "How far?"
He answered in a torn shout, almost a growl,
in a language I had never heard before.
With a jolt of the carriage the candle flame went out.

Saddened by fear
that the king would have no time for music
I journeyed in the dark
deep into the heart of the country,
while the countess sobbed;
I prayed in my last hope that the king
had need of music.

*

All my music is played on black keys.

"Oh dear ancient one . . ." groans the organ
in the archbishop's church below the cliffs of the dead,
"Oh King of salt and steel."

My fingers are armed riders spreading over the plains—
they are women undressing by a window—
they are pigeons scattering from a rooftop—
they are icicles in white sky—

the spaces of nothing between the houses,
which are called the wind.

*

The people in the city are notes
that have taken to themselves
colourful masks of papier maché,
ricepaper, feathers, leather and wood,
and dance.

I left Salzburg
and played music on black keys for the king,
who wanted entertainments instead;
now I have chosen to leave the king, to return to Salzburg,
to exile in the darkness of my self.
The Bishop sneers, but I accept his condemnation
as my own.

Music is a compression at the core
of the colour blue, a clown who trades his smile
for his eyes with a flash of a white-gloved hand,

and only what is past
is.

Tell *that* to the Bishop.

*

The world sits at the dark window,
breathing, and slowly becomes the night.
Nothing watches:
The night sits at a blue pool
and slowly becomes now.

Swallows Flying Above the Salzach

Old cathedrals float down the green river
from walled cities in the mountains,

as once did steamships with cargoes of pine lumber
and tables laid with crystal.

In every window, Mozart can be seen
with a blue bird

of finely blown glass
coated with silver

resting on his fingertips.
Window by window

he blows the bird
onto the waves. Some days

a dozen cathedrals float by.
Mozart is in every one.

When they pass in the night
the cathedrals are black; they bob

through the hearts of eastern cities
like a veil drawn across the eyes

by a woman in love with shadows.
Every day thousands of blue birds flare above the water,

turning and dipping,
fast, as they fly.

Morning Fire

There are cymbals and dancing
on the night lake.

In the villages men wear wooden masks
and fill their pillows with snow.
From a fallow field, Mozart walks in,
followed by crows.

In the blue air before dawn
a crow stands on the stone
sill of each house,
preening its feathers.

Mozart is in a tavern by the river
drinking the last beer.

As the sun pierces the blue fog
the crows lift off house by house,
just before the yellow knife of light
slashes over them,

and spiral high into the sky,
carrying away the dreams
of the people within.

At dawn, Mozart staggers into an alley,
the sun glaring suddenly in his face
like a cardinal placing an ear of wheat
in Mary's hand

as she cradles her golden child
in a cathedral of hand-cut marble
and white stone flowers.

By then the crows are gone
and the streets filled
with morning rivers of fire.
Mozart battles up them alone.

He has been doing this for centuries,
and for centuries people have been
carving masks of wood
to fit their faces perfectly
and to represent what little
they can remember
of their lives.

Every morning they burn away.

The Deciphering of the Code of Time

Kuppenheim

After the wars of religious hate
the children of farmers
were sent to the rivers
that flowed from the forest,
to gather pebbles

which their fathers set in plaster
on the outside wall of the castle
of peacocks and mirrors,
in the dense mathematical patterns
of a Bach fugue—a sombre dirge
for the end of the age of earth
and the beginning of a paradise
of glass and jewels.

That was long past,
in the country of cherry trees and eels,
yet after the wars of human hate
the castle and the river are still there,
a wind that has blown across time.

Today Mozart has awoken for the hundredth time
in a pigeon, his throat banded with jewels,
his feathers glowing with the light of rain.
He sits on the pink sandstone sill
of one of the hundred windows
of the castle's front facade
among the old beech trees,
following the pattern of the stones,

while goldfish swim
in the algal water of pools,
glinting occasionally as they turn
in shafts of sunlight.

After a hundred incarnations
he has uncovered only half of the design
of grief and hope
in one wall of the castle,

but he continues his work,
with his small dark eyes
and his yellow beak. Every afternoon
he flaps down with the others

to eat the yellow grain
children from the village scatter
across the broad black paving stones
of the courtyard.

He has learned
that patience and silence too
are music.

The Room of Mirrors

Schloss Favourite

Mozart is living in the sun,
in halls of gold and mirrors,
in which each candle burns
a thousand times in hallways
of light and given darkness.
There are secret doorways
that lead through the darkness of stone
to the kitchens far below,
where polished copper kettles
hang on iron hooks,
and there are doorways
that lead into blue air.

Sometimes Mozart rows
a thin wooden boat into the blue water
that laps at the shores of the sun,
and leaves a trail of foam from his oars.

He found the building abandoned,
full of smoky wind smelling of potato stalks
burning in black clay fields, and moved in,
and aired out all the rooms. There is one
great hall which he left for the birds.
Birds of all kinds make their homes there.
They perch on gilded chandeliers
and nest on golden cornices.

In the middle of the day,
when the green and blue wind
blows in through empty window frames
like a wave of light separating from matter,
the music of the birds floods the whole sun
and Mozart dances with a thousand shadows,
each one framed in gold.

Noah In Our Time

For his journey across the black sea,
Mozart has sewn a balloon
from an old circus tent
abandoned by gypsies
in an autumn forest
of drifting yellow leaves.

Deep within his hearing
snow is falling.
A wolf paces through the storm,
grey as wood.

On a stone doorstep
a woman with red hair
holds a white candle.

With that flame
Mozart is filling his balloon.

Far from land,
where there is neither day
nor night, only water
rolling over on cold water,
a whale breaches
among waves a hundred feet tall.

As it rises,
the spume of its breath
becomes a tree
with green leaves
through which fly tiny
yellow and red birds.

By morning the balloon is full.
Mozart climbs into the basket
and chops the ropes
with an axe.

As the starlight sinks around her, the woman
with the hair of petunia petals
blows out the flame in her hand,

and on her breath the balloon floats
up off the earth into the blue
and twittering sky,

carrying Mozart, leaning over the edge
of the basket, excited,
waiting for the smell of salt
on the air.

The Speakers

There are points we are willing
and unwilling to cross,

that limit us and set us free
from matter—hard core of starlight:

the dandelion in the core of an apple,
the elk in the glass of the window,

the bear in my fingernails,
the drowning sailor in a door.

From the knife-edge of morning,
that peels the orange sun,

to the frog that leaps from the eyes to the cheek
and clings there, throbbing,

these are words. They do not own you. They
do not push a canoe from shore

as the lake rises out of itself to clutch the rain, and yet
they speak to our listening.

A New City

"To build the city of Dioce whose terraces are the colour of stars."

"4 times was the city rebuilded . . .
now in the mind indestructible."

Ezra Pound

The Sun Glanced Off My Face As If I Were a Mirror of Brass

I was asleep
in a cathedral of red cloth
and stone, in a city
where men, women and children
all wore black dresses
and lived in fear
that the world would pass
through a tiny hole.

Men shaved off their hands,
and did not smile;
in the shadows they hung paintings
from the stone.

I walked from painting to painting.

Without hands
I could not touch them.

The Living City

In the city of Dioce
dolphins surface from the streets,
a cock stands on the steeple,
pink in the morning sun.

In the hour when grass is brought in
from night meadows
and bulls are released
into the squares to feed
on still trembling flowers—
snorting and clattering
over the cobbles—
women sit on rooftop terraces,
drinking cool wine
made of dandelions and oranges.

Sometimes a whale breaks
in front of the church
with a thunderous roar
and the whole section of town
rises and settles
for hours after she dives again.

This is the city that keeps the philosopher's stone.
Its symbol is an emerald-coloured parrot
that has walked straight out of the colour of grass,
still gleaming with the fog of morning.

At times the bird can be seen
as a cloud that fills all the streets at once,
quivering.

At times
there is the patter
of many horses at night
running in the packed sand
by the sea,

while the women sit on their terraces,
stars cascading into their hair.

The City is Famous for Libraries and Houses of Music

In the library of the musicians
there are no books,
no recordings, and no instruments,
yet of all the libraries
it is the most visited. In the long aisles
are stacked rain, stones, rivers, birds
balancing on black, fog-drenched twigs.

Everyone who enters
finds his or her self
standing stock still
in a far aisle
as the sun breaks through mist.

Throughout the library
musicians step forward
slowly,
so as not to frighten their bodies,
touching them at first gently
on the shoulders. When their bodies turn
and recognize their place,
the musicians draw them close
and cradle them.
in arms
that have held the snow
and have not held snow.

Everyone who enters the library enters alone.

No one leaves.

The Highest Peaks

In the city of Dioce
the moon is close
over the shoulder of the land
and covers the entire sky.

The milky mountains
of its highest cordillera
scrape above the roofs
of the houses
as it turns overhead.

When it is full
every stone and every wall,
every tree and flower,
glows like Santorini
above the sea.

Every house in Dioce
encloses a courtyard
planted with lemons and pomegranates.

From these trees clouds of twittering sparrows
rise into the blue sun.

When the cold comes
the birds do not migrate south
where the heat clings to the spines of cacti
and pierces to the cores of stones,

but fly in a vast scintillating swarm,
like butterflies,
onto the plains of the moon.

In the winter nights,
when the starlight crystallises
like frost on a window pane,
spreading night by night
across the sky as the moon wanes—

as if a breath is taking shape out of moisture—
young men

climb golden steeples
with blunderbusses over their shoulders
and thigh-length, hand-sewn
leather boots; they try to grasp the hook of the moon
as it swings by overhead.

At the last moment,
when the moon nears,
its face covered with birds,

a few of the birds swoop off the plains
and through the young men's hair,

and the wind of gravity tugs at them
strongly,

until they let go of the steeples

and fly.

The Water of Life

Water is prized
above the finest wine
and the citizens can tell you
from which stream
on what mountain
the water came,
at what time of day
in which season
it was gathered.

In the space of drinking there is no mind,
no electrical charge
travelling down the squeezed planes of the nerves,
but a single cold pool
lit by the shadowless light of high cloud,
in which the sun burns in every droplet
at once.

The people of the city
are able to taste the stones of a streambed
and know the waters of every stream
in the country.

They say of water that it tastes like memory,
the voice, the essence of words,
a language in itself—in that moment
when the body disappears it speaks;
water tastes of the beginning of the world—
it is the strongest argument
among the philosophers and regents
that the first moment of wonder and lightning
is still here, that all the distances of space
and convolutions of time
are expanding within that moment,
which, in itself, is still infinitesimally small
because there in potential,
realized by drinking water,
untranslatable
into any other language in the world.

With this paradox the philosophers
are content to live, for it is through that paradox
that they can taste water.

Hours after drinking, in the deep of night,
when our dreams walk the streets
and we walk among them
with leaves pressed over our eyes and mouths,
lightning strikes on the plain surrounding the city;
the lightning flashes
reflect off the faces and roofs of all the buildings,
and in that instant of reflection each house is a mirror,
and what it sees is cast out instantly into the world
and is gone—

a whole world in the shape of the houses of the city
travelling outwards among the stars
at the speed of thought,

growing wider and wider as it travels,
until it is as thin and vaporous
as the clouds of the night
and the name of the world.

The Lovers

When the locusts come
in green clouds out of the desert,
people bolt their shutters
and sit in the mauve dark.

If they must walk out
they clench an iron nail
between their teeth,
for the taste of iron
is the exact mirror of the desert;
it is safe passage.

Few people venture out:
as the locusts strike the windows,
a driving rain,
they pace restlessly
between long discussions of snow,
the philosophy of totemism,
and the healing of wounds
with hands laid on forehead
or breast;

except the lovers—
they meet in the loud whirl of locusts;
they crush them underfoot

as they run down the highways,

under the bare trees of the avenues,
away from the city

into the hot stones
and the name of rust.
To be a lover in the city is the most public act.

The regulations of the regents,
the patents of clock makers,
the charts of astronomers,
the stories of merchants and thieves,
are private to lovers—
a sense of personal dissolution—

but the brush of lip,
the curve of breast,
the depths of whisper,
the swell of cock,
are printed in newspapers—
as were headlines announcing victory, treachery,
and speeches from the commanders
in the years of shame.

"This afternoon under the plane tree . . ."
"Your kisses are sparrows in hawthorns in July . . ."
"When I saw you in the dawn light . . ."

The people who read these papers are not lovers;
the lovers have no time to read. They lie together
as the sun streams through the grasslands;
they are inseparable.

When people read the papers
the click of pages turning

reminds them of the arrival of locusts
on a searing August wind.

They read each page
with a tremor of excitement, the grasses
growing in far fields of their fingers
trembling.

The Weight of the World

The roots of the city are deep in stone.
In its branches
ants are used for divination.
Its people
can read the thoughts of colonies
on the grasslands
surrounding the walls—
not immediately, but slowly,
over years: revealing
the complete transparency
of the world.

Thought in any guise is revered
in the city. The ants
are honoured for their immediacy,
their ability to linger,
and their propensity to think
with dreams.

For them there is only space;
all time is present—
a depth to vision. As a demonstration,
punky logs are occasionally set onto open fires.
As carpenter ants
walk out of the wood, across the red-hot coals,
people suddenly feel earth fall away
and space spring up,

and know that it was always there
and carried them.

The Winter City

In winter storms
the city perches on a cliff
over the Irish sea.
Gulls rise and cry
above white teeth of spray.
The door frames
twist. In the windows
there is no glass;
chill sea air
hurls through the rooms,
over faces
of sleepers. Cormorants
cry. Surf pounds at the walls;
spray rises
to the highest towers;
the roar booms down the streets,
slipping, turning.

Winter travellers come by shipwreck
with cries in the night, terrors;
in the blue mouth of morning
ships with torn sails and snapped masts
are driven against the parapets;
the air smells of salt;
the sun is fog: it fills all the streets
with one fire,

revealing the scattered cargoes—
amphorae, blocks of copper and tin,
beads of deep blue glass.
The people are found wet and shivering,
huddled in doorways,
speaking indecipherable tongues.

While they are warmed and fed
in the old quarters,
men rush to the heights
to save the barques and caravelles.
Spray breaks over them.
Ice builds on every surface,
pale blue and white.

In the summer there are no traces of ships
other than long hemp ropes
hanging down the walls.
As shallow white drifts
blow in the nearest streets,
the citizens lie on the sand
that presses against the gates,
close their eyes
and feel their bodies fill with light.

The travellers have not learned so well
the lessons of the world;
they fill so brightly that they vanish.
They are found only at night,
shivering in the open squares
under the planes,
each one alone; they know not from whence they come,
where they have travelled,
what path the light has followed through them

into the city from the world.

It is true that in the city
everyone is a traveller
who travels alone.

Once you have travelled to the city
there is no path through the world
that does not lead through the city
to the roar of the sea.

The Message

From the city
men lead camels
into the shifting sand.

They are watched for hours
from the highest towers

by men in red robes,
until they vanish, tiny,
into the mirroring wall of heat—

then the watchers cry out
with a long, drawn-out wail of joy
sung deep in the throat.

The travellers have hawks on their wrists
and messages in their pockets.
They are on their way
to the king.

The message they bring
is a tiny silver box
that when opened in daylight,
as the sand whips in
off the streets,
contains the sun, and when shut
contains instantaneously
its absence,
which was there before it.

It is the simplest thing in the world,
but also the most inscrutable.

The men let the hawks go free;
the hawks return with empty claws;

while the king is unaware
that a message is on its way
from the world.

The Other City

When the wind blows from the west,
the citizens rush into the square
to feel the rain on their faces
and to see ocean birds
soaring high and alone,
small specks against a distant sky.

When the wind burns from the east
the windows are shut
against the sand—
it drives into the eyes
and fills the glasses in the cupboards;
the weather is hot;
everyone is agitated.

When the wind eases from the south
the citizens rush
to stand under the planes
that line the avenues,
to feel them tug at their roots
as the sky enters the earth.

When the wind rages from the north
the citizens slip on bright clothes
and haul their pianos out
to the top of a distant mountain—

they set them up
in starlight
and play them like desert grass
soughing in wind,

for that is how the city began

and there is a saying
in the markets

that that is how it will end.
The city of Dioce

is a rich city
and is not to be confused
with a city of merchants
or thieves,

for it is rich in origins
and in departures;

when the wind is still
and the air lies in the streets like crystal,

citizens of the city
move through it at will.

It is a sight to see white bullocks
pulling heavy wooden carts

up dusty slopes,
their muscles cording,
and people walking alongside
laughing and singing,

but it is perhaps a greater sight
to see them come back down
the next day,
the people sleeping,
lying in the carts
alongside pianos,
and the bullocks racing down,
driverless,
the carts swinging out on the corners,
over cliffs,
music springing up from keys
as the wagons clump over stones,
like the water of a brook
running bright blue and silver
down into a valley
from the clouds.

It is a sound the people never hear,
but it rides with them always,
deep within their hearing.